Offer It Up

Reflection Journal

Offer It Up

Reflection Journal

For use with the book...

Offer It Up

A story of faith, one man's battle with cancer, and a witness to how God uses our suffering to help others

Jeff Krohn

Copyright © 2024 by Jeff Krohn

All rights reserved. Except for quotations, no part of this book may be reproduced or transmitted in any form or by any means, electronic or mechanical, including photocopying, recording, uploading to the Internet, or by any information storage and retrieval system, without written permission from the author.

For more information or permissions, contact four.saints.publishing@gmail.com

All scripture quotations are from The Catholic Edition of the Revised Standard Version of the Bible, copyright © 1965, 1966 National Council of the Churches of Christ in the United States of America. Used by permission. All rights reserved worldwide.

Information on Exodus 90 courtesy exodus90.com

Exodus 90

Cover design by Jeff Krohn

RELIGION / Christian Living / Spiritual Growth

RELIGION / Christian Living / Inspirational

ISBN: 979-8-9922128-1-5

1 3 5 7 9 10 8 6 4 2

First edition

Introduction

This reflection journal is designed to pair with the book *Offer It Up: A story of faith, one man's battle with cancer, and a witness to how God uses our suffering to help others.*

Each chapter of the book is briefly summarized on the left-hand page, then the three reflection questions from each chapter are presented on the following pages with ample space for journaling.

1

An Invitation

In the opening chapter, Jeff recalls a pivotal moment when the sudden death of a 47-year-old acquaintance shook him, prompting reflections on the fragility of life and the need to deepen his faith. Realizing his own spiritual complacency, he felt the timing was providential when a friend invited him to join Exodus 90, a rigorous 90-day spiritual exercise for men focused on fasting, prayer, self-denial, and fraternity.

Although the program was challenging—with commitments like cold showers, daily prayer, and denial of worldly pleasures—it transformed Jeff's life. He developed a stronger prayer life, discovered resilience in doing difficult things, and forged meaningful friendships, particularly with the friend who invited him, who became like a brother.

Jeff reflects on how this experience prepared him for the trials he would face years later, equipping him with faith, discipline, and a supportive community to endure life's challenges.

An Invitation

Have there been any significant moments in your life when you were called to renew or deepen your faith? Was there a particular person or group that inspired you to start taking your faith more seriously?

Offer It Up

How does the awareness of life's fragility affect the way you live your daily life and prioritize your spiritual and personal growth? What changes can you make today to live with more purpose and awareness?

An Invitation

Have you ever reflected on the reality of your own death (memento mori)? Are you prepared for it spiritually and practically? Have you told your loved ones, both family and friends, what they mean to you before it is too late? If not, why not?

Offer It Up

An Invitation

2

The Journey Begins

In this chapter, Jeff shares how a routine physical unexpectedly led to a prostate cancer diagnosis at age 48, which is unusual at that age.

Initially, the gravity of the diagnosis didn't fully register, but Jeff struggled with feelings of frustration, disbelief, and anger at having what he considered an "old man's disease." He shared the news cautiously, informing only his wife, kids, and closest friends. His wife's history of losing her mother to cancer deepened her fears, while Jeff grappled with embarrassment and stress.

Despite his initial resistance, encouragement from his best friend and scripture reminders about trusting God helped Jeff begin processing the diagnosis. This marked the start of an emotional and spiritual journey toward acceptance and faith.

The Journey Begins

When has a routine event turned into a pivotal moment in your life? How do you see God's hand in these moments?

OFFER IT UP

How can vulnerability and openness within a supportive community of friends and family help us navigate life's trials?

How do you see the connection between your spiritual life and your physical well-being? How might a deepened faith provide strength during times of physical or emotional hardship?

Offer It Up

The Journey Begins

3

Wrestling with Trust

In this chapter, Jeff shares the emotional and spiritual journey he experienced after his initial diagnosis. Struggling to accept his diagnosis, he grappled with feelings of frustration, questioning why God would allow him to face such a challenge so young. A visit to his church's adoration chapel became a turning point, as he prayed for trust in God and unexpectedly found clarity and peace through the words of a hymn being practiced on the organ.

The biopsy results revealed a less aggressive cancer which could be managed through active surveillance. While Jeff felt relieved, his wife, deeply shaped by her mother's cancer experience, was still concerned.

As Jeff shared his diagnosis more openly, he received prayers and encouragement, which strengthened his faith. This period of relative stability allowed him to grow emotionally and spiritually, preparing him for future challenges in his journey.

Have you ever experienced a time when trusting God was difficult due to life's challenges? How did you work through your doubts?

OFFER IT UP

How has God shown you answers in unexpected ways? Are you open to seeing His hand in your life?

When you pray, do you take the time to listen to God's response? Most people do not literally hear a voice when they say God spoke to them. In what ways do you experience His voice?

Offer It Up

Wrestling with Trust

4

A Friend's Suffering

The summer after he was diagnosed with cancer, Jeff faced the devastating news that his best friend's 18-month-old son had suffered a severe choking accident. After rushing to support his friend and his family at the hospital, Jeff witnessed the deep anguish in their eyes and struggled with his own pain and questions about God's plan.

Later that night, overwhelmed by the situation, Jeff broke down in tears in his car, reflecting on the heartbreak he had seen and the innocence of the boy's three-year-old brother asking when his sibling would wake up.

Desperate to help, Jeff prayed on his way home, asking God to let him take on some of his friend's suffering. He felt called to offer his own cancer as redemptive suffering, uniting it with Christ's for his friend's sake. When the child passed away two days later, Jeff leaned on his faith in the Catholic teaching of redemptive suffering, finding purpose in his pain through Christ's salvific mission.

Have you ever experienced a time when you were able to find meaning or purpose in your suffering? How can you deepen your understanding of suffering as a way to participate in God's plan or offer support to others?

Offer It Up

Would you be willing to offer your suffering for someone you love? What about for an acquaintance? What about for a stranger?

In what ways have you been inspired by others who are facing challenges, and how does that shape your approach to your own struggles?

Offer It Up

A Friend's Suffering

5

An Unexpected Cross

Jeff recounts the emotional and spiritual journey leading up to his prostate cancer surgery. A routine checkup revealed his PSA levels had doubled, signaling the need for immediate surgery. Shocked by the sudden escalation, Jeff wrestled with his emotions but leaned on his faith and the support of his family and community.

Sharing the news with his wife and children, Jeff maintained a positive approach to avoid overwhelming them, though he later learned how deeply his diagnosis affected them.

Turning to prayer, he realized the timing of his worsening condition aligned perfectly with his offering of redemptive suffering for a friend, causing him to realize this was likely part of God's plan.

Humbled by the outpouring of prayers from his parish and beyond, Jeff saw God's hand in the situation. Preparing for surgery, he focused on family, set his affairs in order, and sought spiritual strength through the sacrament of Anointing of the Sick, finding peace in God's perfect timing.

What cross are you currently carrying, and how can you invite God to walk alongside you?

What does friendship look like? What do close friends do for each other?

How do you recognize or interpret signs of God's hand in your life? How might sharing your experiences impact others?

Offer It Up

An Unexpected Cross

6

UNDER THE KNIFE

In this chapter, Jeff recounts the details of his cancer surgery. The procedure turned out to be far more complex than anticipated. Originally planned as a two-hour operation, it extended to nearly five hours due to unexpected cancer growth and the surgeon's meticulous effort to prevent damage to surrounding tissue.

While Jeff recovered in the hospital for two nights, he reflected on the challenges of healing and leaned on his faith. The pathology results brought good news: the cancer had been fully removed, and nearby lymph nodes showed no signs of spread. This was a significant relief.

Although he initially felt isolated during recovery, the outpouring of prayers and support, particularly from his best friend who prayed for him throughout a trip to Rome, reminded Jeff of the incredible blessings of family, friendship, faith, and community.

In what ways can we feel God's presence through relationships? How might your faith be strengthened by the support of others in difficult times?

How does the concept of offering our struggles for the benefit of others impact your perspective on suffering? What are other ways you might transform hardships into acts of faith?

How can reflecting on your blessings reshape your mindset in challenging times?

Offer It Up

Under the Knife

7

From Hope to Uncertainty

In this chapter, Jeff reflects on his post-surgery recovery, which went smoothly but was marked by boredom and frustration due to activity restrictions. Initially encouraged by his PSA levels decreasing as expected, Jeff faced an unsettling turn when another PSA test revealed the levels had plateaued. A call from his surgeon confirmed the worst: lingering concerns about cancer.

The doctor recommended a cutting-edge PSMA PET scan to detect potential metastasis. Fascinated with the technology yet anxious, Jeff underwent the scan and received the results on the drive home. The phrase "metastatic nodal disease" confirmed that the cancer had spread to his lymph nodes, leaving Jeff overwhelmed with fear and uncertainty.

Struggling to process the news, Jeff wrestled with how to tell his wife, knowing the weight it would carry. He eventually shared the diagnosis, realizing they faced a new battle together. Anchored by faith, Jeff held onto the belief that God's plan would bring meaning to this struggle.

How do you typically respond when faced with difficult or unexpected challenges?

_____
_____
_____
_____
_____
_____
_____
_____
_____
_____
_____
_____
_____
_____
_____
_____
_____
_____
_____
_____

OFFER IT UP

What role does your faith play in helping you navigate times of uncertainty? How can you draw closer to God during these times?

How might you create a "spiritual toolkit" to help you navigate times of difficulty and uncertainty?

Offer It Up

From Hope to Uncertainty

8

INTO BATTLE

Jeff describes the work of assembling a world-class medical team after learning his prostate cancer had metastasized. His surgeon referred him to a trusted oncologist, who advocated for an aggressive treatment plan combining androgen deprivation therapy (ADT) with chemotherapy, recognizing the challenges of treating aggressive cancer in a younger patient.

During his first appointment with the oncologist, Jeff grappled with the prognosis: an 85% chance of survival, leaving a sobering 15% risk. The phrase in the treatment plan, "The goal of treatment is to prolong life," further drove home the seriousness of his condition, emphasizing the need to fight relentlessly.

Despite the daunting reality, Jeff resolved to begin treatment immediately, relying on his faith to conquer fear. While he wrestled with frustration, confusion, and anger, his unwavering trust in God and the steadfast support of his wife, kids, and community gave him strength. Jeff embraced the battle with hope, faith, and determination.

His wife's unwavering support and daily prayers became a source of strength as he prepared to fight cancer head-on, determined to face the storm with courage and faith.

Do you believe that bad things can't happen to you? Or are you the opposite and think that only bad things happen to you? Where do you think the right balance is?

How does your faith in the resurrection of Jesus shape the way you view your life and your future, especially when facing the reality of death? How can this eternal perspective influence how you live today?

How can you see God's hand in the people and circumstances that come into your life, especially in times when you feel most vulnerable or uncertain?

Offer It Up

Into Battle

9

THE FIRST DOSE

Jeff recounts the preparations and experiences surrounding his first chemotherapy treatment. A pre-treatment gathering reminded him of the significant support he had. Despite initial excitement and determination to begin treatment, the reality of chemotherapy quickly set in.

During the first session, Jeff sat in the treatment room, surrounded by others in varying stages of illness. As the chemotherapy flowed, he found humor in the nurse donning protective gear for the same chemicals entering his veins. Ice packs on his hands and feet to reduce side effects were the worst physical discomfort, while the surreal realization of his stage 4 cancer weighed heavily.

That evening, camaraderie with friends brought much-needed levity. Their dark humor, though irreverent, reinforced bonds and helped him face treatment with a positive mindset. He continued to offer his suffering for his friend, trusting in God's plan. Grateful for his community, he left energized to tackle the challenges ahead.

What is your reaction when you need to start something difficult? Do you dread it? Do you avoid it? Do you attack it head on?

Offer It Up

When you face a challenge, do you bring it to God in prayer? Do you ask for His help? Do you get mad at Him?

Can laughter, even in the face of suffering, be a form of trust in God's ability to bring light into the darkness?

Offer It Up

The First Dose

10

Chemo, Covid, and Crosses

After his first chemotherapy treatment, Jeff tested positive for Covid. Despite a quick recovery, it was a stark reminder of his vulnerable, immunocompromised state. The chemotherapy side effects soon emerged, including numbness in his fingers, nausea, and a diminished sense of taste. These signs underscored the gravity of his journey, leaving Jeff in a reflective and somber mood.

Acknowledging his struggles, Jeff considered others' hardships—friends, fellow parishioners, and even children facing cancer—realizing the importance of perspective and empathy. Through prayer, he embraced the notion that everyone bears unique crosses, and that mutual support can lighten the load.

A turning point came when Jeff's best friend accompanied him to a chemotherapy session, offering humor and companionship on a difficult day. This act of kindness reinforced the power of friendship and faith, reminding Jeff that God works through others to provide strength and solace during life's trials.

How does the presence of suffering in your life make you more aware of the suffering of others? How does your faith shape the way you view and endure suffering?

Offer It Up

How do you accept help or encouragement from others when facing trials? How might this deepen your relationships?

What practical steps can you take to strengthen your spiritual and emotional resilience in times of trial?

Offer It Up

Chemo, Covid, and Crosses

11

JOY IN THE JOURNEY

In this chapter, Jeff shares his journey through chemotherapy while reflecting on the challenges, community, and blessings that emerged during his treatment. Genetic testing revealed he carries the HOXB13 mutation, increasing his sons' risk of prostate cancer but sparing his daughters from heightened breast cancer risks. As chemotherapy progressed, Jeff experienced worsening side effects, including hair loss and loss of taste, underscoring the seriousness of his condition.

Despite the hardships, Jeff maintained a joyful attitude, finding strength in his faith and the supportive community at the treatment center. He observed the silent suffering around him but recognized that Christian joy carried him through.

A surprise 50th birthday party, thoughtfully planned by his wife and friends, became a celebration of life, friendships, and the end of chemotherapy.

Jeff expressed deep gratitude for the love and prayers of those around him, acknowledging the power of friendship, faith, and shared burdens in sustaining hope and resilience.

It's been said that we make time for the people who are important to us no matter how busy we are. How well do you live this with both your family and your friends?

Offer It Up

How can joy and gratitude transform your experience of life's challenges?

How do you share joy with others even in times of personal struggle?

Offer It Up

Joy in the Journey

12

A Lonely Fight

In this chapter, Jeff reflects on the isolating experience of battling cancer, even amidst tremendous support. The constant presence of the disease, its treatments, and their life-altering effects weigh heavily on him, yet he finds solace in faith, family, and friendships.

His wife and children provide steadfast encouragement, while friends offer prayers, heartfelt notes, and unwavering support. Jeff acknowledges the transformative power of Christian community, realizing that God's love often manifests through others.

Moments of deep gratitude intermingle with the physical and emotional struggles of cancer. Prayers from strangers and friends, some shared in unconventional ways, remind him that he is not alone. He reflects on the importance of fostering relationships, recognizing how friends' faith can lift up and sustain people during trials, much like in the biblical story of the paralytic healed through his friends' faith.

Jeff challenges readers to cultivate strong, loving connections, emphasizing that Christian community provides the strength to endure life's inevitable hardships.

In what ways have you seen God's presence through the support of others during difficult times?

What role does prayer play in your journey through suffering? How do you discern God's answers, especially when they are not what you expect?

What roles do friendships and community play in your life? How do you nurture those relationships?

Offer It Up

A Lonely Fight

13

An Unintended Witness

Jeff reflects on the profound impact his cancer journey has had on others, as well as the spiritual challenges and insights he has experienced along the way.

Though he initially dismissed comments about his inspiring example, repeated affirmations from friends, strangers, and coworkers made him realize the strength of his faith and its visibility to others. Encounters with people moved by his perseverance, including those who found healing or inspiration through his story, humbled him and highlighted how God can work through personal suffering.

Jeff also wrestles with the unanswered prayers for healing, ultimately recognizing that God's responses often serve a greater purpose, whether strengthening him, inspiring others, or providing opportunities for redemptive suffering. He shares moments of spiritual clarity during prayer, including a message from God to embrace his cross as Jesus did. Despite struggles with physical and emotional pain, Jeff's faith and prayer sustain him, reminding him of God's love and the power of Christian community.

How do you respond when others see qualities in you that you don't see in yourself?

Offer It Up

When someone compliments you, do you feel unworthy? Do you feel like you don't live up to how they see you? Is this humility, or something else?

In what ways might God be using your struggles or challenges to inspire those around you? How can you turn to God to understand His purpose for your life?

Offer It Up

An Unintended Witness

14

ONE STEP CLOSER

In this chapter, Jeff transitions to the next phase of his cancer treatment after completing chemotherapy. Faced with ongoing challenges, he undergoes a second surgery and begins androgen deprivation therapy (ADT), a demanding treatment with numerous side effects. ADT brings mood swings, fatigue, muscle atrophy, and hot flashes, further complicating Jeff's daily life. Despite these struggles, his wife's support and practical advice help him navigate this difficult time.

Radiation therapy becomes the next step, carrying its own risks and challenges. After careful consideration, Jeff and his medical team decide to delay radiation slightly, allowing him to take a long-planned trip with his best friend. The trip provides much-needed respite, laughter, and normalcy before Jeff embarks on eight weeks of daily radiation sessions.

After completing radiation, Jeff rings the celebratory bell, marking another milestone. Surrounded by family and friends, he reflects on the blessings in his life and gives thanks for God's presence throughout his journey.

What role does patience play in your faith, especially when dealing with long and difficult challenges?

How do humor and friendship serve as a reminder of God's love and support in hard moments?

In what ways can you celebrate the milestones in a long, difficult journey with gratitude, knowing that every step is part of God's plan for you?

Offer It Up

One Step Closer

15

DECIDING TO LIVE

In this chapter, Jeff reflects on the long and challenging "home stretch" of his cancer treatment. With surgery, chemotherapy, and radiation behind him, he faces thirteen more months of hormone therapy, bringing side effects like mood swings, fatigue, insomnia, and hot flashes. Despite feeling physically and emotionally drained, Jeff resolves to push through, refusing to let cancer define his life.

A false alarm in his PSA levels briefly suggests a potential cancer recurrence, but further tests confirm it was a lab error, bringing immense relief. Another scare arises with numbness in his leg, initially suspected to be cancer spreading to his spine. After a nerve-wracking wait, tests reveal it is only spinal arthritis, likely caused by previous treatments—not cancer.

These experiences prompt Jeff to reassess his outlook, focusing on living fully rather than as a cancer patient. Inspired to push his limits, he embraces new challenges, like joining a bootcamp workout, finding renewed mental strength, and reaffirming his faith in God's plan.

In what ways do you see God working in your life even when circumstances seem overwhelming?

Have you ever had a moment where you had to accept a reality that was different than what you had hoped for? How did you find peace in that?

How can you "push through" difficult circumstances while also giving yourself the grace to heal and rest—physically, emotionally, and spiritually?

Offer It Up

Deciding to Live

16

FAITH IN THE WAITING

In this final chapter, Jeff reflects on the conclusion of his cancer treatment and the uncertain journey ahead. There is no triumphant ending—the process quietly transitions into a period of monitoring and recovery, with no definitive declaration of being cancer-free.

Jeff learns that it will take ten years of regular PSA tests and monitoring to determine if the cancer is cured. Each test brings the anticipation of either relief or the possibility of recurrence.

As treatment ends, Jeff grapples with his identity shifting from "cancer patient" to "cancer survivor," struggling to redefine himself beyond the journey that has shaped him for three years. While he acknowledges he will never be the same physically, emotionally, or spiritually, he sees God's hand in his transformation.

Expressing deep gratitude for his family, friends, faith, and the ability to offer his suffering for others, Jeff resolves to surrender more fully to God's will, trusting in His guidance for the next chapter of his life.

How can waiting become a time of spiritual growth rather than frustration? What practices or disciplines help you remain faithful during these times?

When you reflect on God's presence, how have you experienced His love and peace in ways that you didn't expect?

How can you help others carry their crosses, even if you're carrying one of your own?

Offer It Up

Faith in the Waiting

Extra Journal Pages

Offer It Up

Offer It Up

Offer It Up

Offer It Up

Offer It Up

Offer It Up

Offer It Up

Offer It Up

Offer It Up

Offer It Up

Offer It Up

Offer It Up

Offer It Up

Offer It Up

Offer It Up

Offer It Up

Offer It Up

Offer It Up

Offer It Up

Offer It Up

Offer It Up

Offer It Up

www.ingramcontent.com/pod-product-compliance
Lightning Source LLC
Chambersburg PA
CBHW030446100526
44580CB00001B/4